Sacred
Cycle

Mary McDonald

Our Sacred Cycle

A Workbook to Reclaim Your Period from PMS & PMDD

Mary McDonald

Microcosm Publishing
Portland, OR | Cleveland, OH

Our Sacred Cycle

A Workbook to Reclaim Your Period from PMS & PMDD

Part of the DIY Series

© **Mary McDonald, December 2024**

This edition © Microcosm Publishing, 2024

First Edition, 3,000 copies, first published

ISBN 9781648412103

This is Microcosm #928

Designed by Joe Biel

Illustrated by Mary McDonald

Edited by Kandi Zeller

For a catalog, write or visit:

Microcosm Publishing

2752 N Williams Ave.

Portland, OR 97227

(503)799-2698

Microcosm.Pub

All the news that's fit to print at www.Microcosm.Pub/Newsletter

Get more copies of this book at www.Microcosm.Pub/SacredCycle

Find more work by Mary McDonald at www.Microcosm.Pub/MaryMcDonald

Did you know that you can buy our books directly from us at sliding scale rates? Support a small, independent publisher and pay less than Amazon's price at **www.Microcosm.Pub.**

To join the ranks of high-class stores that feature Microcosm titles, talk to your rep: In the U.S. **COMO** (Atlantic), **ABRAHAM** (Midwest), **BOB BARNETT** (Texas, Oklahoma, Arkansas, Louisiana), **IMPRINT** (Pacific), **TURNAROUND** (UK), **UTP/MANDA** (Canada), **NEWSOUTH** (Australia/New Zealand), **Observatoire** (Africa, Europe), **IPR** (Middle East), **Yvonne Chau** (Southeast Asia), **HarperCollins** (India), **Everest/B.K. Agency** (China), **Tim Burland** (Japan/Korea), and **FAIRE** in the gift trade.

Global labor conditions are bad, and our roots in industrial Cleveland in the 70s and 80s made us appreciate the need to treat workers right. Therefore, our books are MADE IN THE USA and printed on post-consumer paper.

MICROCOSM PUBLISHING

MICROCOSM PUBLISHING is Portland's most diversified publishing house and distributor, with a focus on the colorful, authentic, and empowering. Our books and zines have put your power in your hands since 1996, equipping readers to make positive changes in their lives and in the world around them. Microcosm emphasizes skill-building, showing hidden histories, and fostering creativity through challenging conventional publishing wisdom with books and bookettes about DIY skills, food, bicycling, gender, self-care, and social justice. What was once a distro and record label started by Joe Biel in a drafty bedroom was determined to be *Publishers Weekly*'s fastest-growing publisher of 2022 and #3 in 2023, and is now among the oldest independent publishing houses in Portland, OR, and Cleveland, OH. Biel is also the winner of PubWest's Innovator Award in 2024. We are a politically moderate, centrist publisher in a world that has inched to the right for the past 80 years.

Contents

Message from the Author

Being in our bodies doesn't have to be a nightmare, but I didn't always know that. Throughout my adolescence and twenties, I experienced major emotional episodes that occurred every month or so. Triggered by physical discomfort, I would become so irritable I'd scream at anyone near me. I would have episodes where everything felt so meaningless that I wouldn't get out of bed for days. It hurt my relationships and self-esteem. No matter how much yoga and meditation I practiced, these dark days always returned.

I wanted help. My doctors consistently misdiagnosed me with bipolar disorder and major depressive disorder. They prescribed me medicine that didn't help. There were times I felt so hopeless and confused about why I wasn't getting better that I believed I didn't want to live.

Finally, when I was 28, someone told me about premenstrual dysphoric disorder (PMDD). I had all the eleven symptoms listed in the Diagnostic and Statistical Manual of Mental Disorders (DSM-5).[1] It was relieving to know I wasn't alone, but also frustrating to think that it took me a decade to realize that my emotional episodes only happened before my period.

I ended up dedicating my graduate school research towards better understanding PMDD and the therapeutic

---

1 *Diagnostic and Statistical Manual of Mental Disorders: DSM-5.* 5th ed., American Psychiatric Association, 2013.

treatments of it. In the process, I listened to what my body and emotional symptoms were speaking to me, and I discovered that I was not mentally ill. I was experiencing valid emotional responses to having a body that had been shamed, misunderstood, and abused in the context of my culture.

After doing my own therapy where I explored the feelings I held in my body, I started having a consistent period for the first time in my life. My "mental illness" no longer felt like a mental illness, and I even began to appreciate being in my body. As I went on to speak and share about my experience and research, many other menstruators (i.e. people who have a period, regardless of their gender identity), reported how being educated on their cycle began to transform them too.

This education and wisdom should not be withheld. It should be passed on. So, I decided to combine my knowledge from research, a decade long teaching career, my own personal therapy, and my psychotherapy practice to create this workbook for you.

Introduction: Wisdom of the Womb

*I*n a culture where the menstruating body is mistreated, misunderstood, and neglected, many menstruators have lost sight of their power. When a young menstruator first gets their period, there is no celebration of their remarkable new ability to create life. Parents and teachers rarely pass on the wisdom of the menstruating body. Menstruators aren't taught how their body joins with the rhythm of the moon and the earth's seasons.

Instead, menstruators learn how to hide their blood. They learn to feel shame around their bleeding body, their mood swings, and their accentuated breasts and hips. This shame is a result of a culture that constantly whispers, "Keep parts of yourself hidden."

Many menstruators have become conditioned to sever the connection between their mind and body so that they can follow societal standards expected of them. Male-dominant, or patriarchal, society pressures the menstruating body to be kept under control, consistent, and predictable. These pressures contradict the needs of a menstruating body. And when the body's needs are ignored, a menstruator cannot learn the wisdom that their body seeks to share.

Menstruators carry a sacred womb with a sacred cycle that helps to sustain life on this planet. Yet, the menstrual cycle is associated with frustration and pain, rather than gratitude and compassion. The emotions and sensations triggered by menstrual hormones, despite what patriarchal culture has communicated, are not "crazy" or something to ignore or be ashamed of. They can be embraced and channeled towards creative projects and personal discovery. The activities in this book are here to assist you in that process.

A Sacred Journey

There are four phases of the menstrual cycle that you will begin to track: the menstrual (bleeding out the uterine lining), follicular (egg development), ovulatory (egg release), and luteal (uterine lining buildup) phases. These phases correlate to four psychological experiences: Release (emotional catharsis), Renewal (emotional expansion), Call (emotional redirection), and Descent (emotional deepening).

In any movie you watch or book you read, the character that transforms into a hero or heroine always is called towards an adventure, descends into a period of trials and tribulations, sacrifices old parts of themselves, and comes out renewed. For thousands of years, myths and literature have told us about characters that go through a journey where they must descend into darkness and suffering so that they can emerge as an embodied and empowered version of themselves. The process of transformation is almost innate to human nature. It's an archetypal pattern.

Ancient Mesopotamian mythology tells the story of Queen Inanna, who was called to descend into the underworld. There, she was stripped of everything she had. She sacrificed parts of herself that she had been attached to so that she could return as a wiser, humbled, and more conscious version of herself. The story of Inanna has been told for thousands of years, and stories today continue to follow this same cycle to depict a character's transformation. More recently, characters like Elsa in Frozen or Katniss in Hunger Games were both called towards an inner descent that led them to become a more empowered, goddess-like version of themselves.

The menstruating body guides you through this archetypal journey towards self-expansion and transformation if you learn to catch and trust the flow. If you do, you will find that each cycle is your own mini-journey that guides you to descend inward and sacrifice what no longer serves you. This journey will lead you closer and closer to your authentic self.

How to Use This Book

As you read, you will be empowered with information about how your behaviors, urges, and emotions may be influenced by your menstrual cycle. You will be guided through activities that increase your mind-body awareness so that you can create a life that is aligned with the fluctuating needs of your menstruating body.

To begin living in tune with your cycle, follow these steps:

Begin by reading "Cycle One: Get to Know your Flow" on page 20.

When you start your next period, read "The Release" on page 23. Then complete the activity on pages 27-30.

Choose a word to describe what you chose to emotionally release during your menstrual phase. Record this word inside a blood drop on page 31.

When you finish bleeding, read "The Renewal" on page 32 and complete the activity on pages 35-37.

Choose a word to describe what was emotionally renewed during your follicular phase. Record this word on a root of the tree on page 38.

About a week and a half later, or halfway through your cycle, read "The Call" on page 39. Complete the activity on pages 42-45.

Choose a word to describe what you were called towards during ovulation. Record this word in the voice of the conch shell on page 46.

After ovulation, or a week before you get your period (whichever is easier for you to track), read "The Descent" on page 47 and complete the activity on pages 53-55.

Choose a word to describe what you descended into during your luteal phase. Record this word in the whirlpool on page 56.

Repeat the steps for your following five cycles, using the corresponding Release, Renewal, Call, and Descent readings and activities for each cycle chapter.

When you have finished all six cycles, reflect on your journey. Complete the concluding activity on page 151.

If you do not have a consistent period and you find it especially difficult to track your phases, try to follow the phases of this book with the phases of the moon: "The Release" during the waxing moon (as it is becoming full), "The Renewal" during the full moon, "The Call" during the waning moon (as it is becoming darker), and "The Descent" during the new moon.

Along the way, you will also be prompted to record (as best you can) the day of your cycle that each phase occurs. Keep in mind that developing a longer-term practice of tracking is critical in learning to maintain a lifestyle that is in harmony with your body. I recommend you use your own calendar, a cycle tracking app (Stardust is a great option), or a phone or computer calendar to track the phases of your cycle.

If you notice that you are having abnormally long, heavy, frequent, or painful periods, or no period at all, it is recommended that you see a doctor to identify or rule out potentially more serious conditions. These symptoms may point towards thyroid issues, ovarian cysts, an iron deficit, or medical issues that could require immediate attention. Irregular cycles could also mean that your body is in perimenopause: this is when the body has irregular periods before officially hitting menopause.

Additionally, there are many resources that discuss how to eat, supplement, and exercise to support your menstrual cycle. *Woman Code* by Alisa Vitti is a great place to start. *Our Sacred Cycle*, on the other hand, takes a therapeutic, emotional approach, guiding you to exercise your mind with the rhythm of your body.

One other important note: Know that the work you will do throughout this book may not always be easy or fun. It may challenge your thinking and illuminate the sides of yourself you would prefer to ignore. Have compassion for yourself through this process and acknowledge the strength it takes to do what you are doing.

Honoring the sacred menstrual cycle is a rebellious act against a society that has oppressed the menstruating body. It is radical to give attention to it, rather than neglect, numb, or become angry about it. If you commit to the process, you might learn to love and connect with a mind-body force that can birth life—literally and creatively—within yourself. It may be the key that unlocks the door to achieving your goals. You have the wisdom within yourself, but you may not yet have been given the tools to listen to it.

Cycle One: Get to Know Your Flow

The menstrual cycle guides the body through four phases, with the purpose of maintaining fertility and potentially creating new life. To outline a complicated physiological process briefly (it will be explained more thoroughly as you read on), these phases are described simply below:

Phase 1—The Menstrual Phase: Day 1 of your cycle. The uterine lining is shed and expelled from your vagina. Your body is swollen and worn out.

Phase 2—The Follicular Phase: Follicles in your ovaries develop eggs. Your body feels refreshed and energetic after just finishing a period.

Phase 3—The Ovulatory Phase: An egg releases out of the dominant follicle in your ovaries. The egg travels down your fallopian tube and towards the uterus. You may start to feel a subtle shift in your body, like mild cramping or more water retention.

Phase 4—The Luteal Phase: Your uterine lining builds up, your body retains water, you become bloated, and so many other side effects occur—all so that your body can begin creating a home for a fetus. If the egg wasn't fertilized, the cycle starts again.

The hormones that are released during each phase of the cycle influence physical sensations, emotions, and mood. Hormones strengthen certain emotional abilities and weaken others. When menstruators can catch their hormonal rhythm, they enter a journey towards personal growth and emotional expansion. When menstruators consciously follow the journey of release, renewal, call towards inspiration, and descent inward, their mind and soul become ripe with new possibility. This is the journey that leads to transformation and growth:

Phase 1—The Release: Your blood's release signals you to consider if you need to let anything go along with your blood. If you have been clinging to an unhelpful thought pattern, an old habit, or an expectation of yourself that no longer serves you, it is time to release it.

Phase 2—The Renewal: During this phase, your ovaries create eggs and, in that process, your hormones can help you create whatever you set your mind to.

Phase 3—The Call: This surge of hormones may redirect your attention away from your Phase 2 tasks (pursuing a mate, planning a party, completing a work task, etc.). This phase calls you to refocus your attention, likely towards your emotional well-being.

Phase 4—The Descent: Your body retains water, bloats, and builds up a uterine lining. The physical tension you experience during this phase brings you the power of inner sensitivity.

Unfortunately, instead of experiencing the above cycle as empowering, menstruators often learn behaviors throughout their life that cause them to resist this journey towards personal creativity. They may try to stay focused on one goal for the entire cycle. They may try to do the same exercise every single day. Or they may forget to take moments to themselves to recharge. Many menstruators feel forced to follow societal standards, rather than their own personal values. Societal standards are impossible to keep up with and weaken the fertility of the soul.

But it doesn't have to be this way. This book will accompany you through six of your menstrual cycles. It will guide you to accept the call of your body and follow whatever journey it takes you on.

The Release: Menstrual Phase

Cycle Day # 1

Your menstrual phase might start with blood filling up your underwear or just some light brown spotting. You might also experience painful cramping in your lower abdomen. Of course, it isn't fun to have to manage blood and pain, but these symptoms are a sign that you've begun a new cycle. Yay!

As you bleed, you might feel so tired that all you want to do is lie in bed and watch shows. Give yourself permission; your body is healing. It is having an inflammatory response to repair your womb, like the experience of having just been injured and needing to rest.

Studies show that, during this phase, the part of your brain in charge of processing your inner mental state becomes activated and your attention turns towards your memories and fantasies for the future.[2] Meanwhile, the part of your brain in charge of cognitive functioning and carrying out tasks weakens. So, consider giving yourself a few days to reflect on the last few weeks and dream about what is to come. There is no reason to try to fight against your mind. Let your body recover from its previous cycle, and let your mind recover from whatever challenges you have recently faced.

The Timeline

The first day that you bleed is the first day of your new cycle. On average, menstruation lasts 3–7 days. If you are pregnant, the uterine lining will stay intact as a fetus grows, meaning you will not get your period. Late periods can happen even when you are not pregnant. That is okay. Late periods might suggest that your cycle is responding or adapting to something new in your environment, such as change in diet, exercise, or sexual activity.

---

2 See Belinda Pletzer, Ti-Anni Harris, Andrea Scheuringer, and Esmeralda Hidalgo-Lopez, "The Cycling Brain: Menstrual Cycle Related Fluctuations in Hippocampal and Fronto-Striatal Activation and Connectivity during Cognitive Tasks," *Neuropsychopharmacology* 44, no. 11 (2019): 1867–75, as well as Esmeralda Hidalgo-Lopez, Peter Zeidman, Ti-Anni Harris, Adeel Razi, and Belinda Pletzer, "Spectral Dynamic Causal Modelling in Healthy Women Reveals Brain Connectivity Changes along the Menstrual Cycle," *Communications Biology* 4, no. 1 (2021): 954 and Stephanie C. Reed, Frances R. Levin, and Suzette M. Evans, "Changes in Mood, Cognitive Performance and Appetite in the Late Luteal and Follicular Phases of the Menstrual Cycle in Women With and Without PMDD (Premenstrual Dysphoric Disorder)," *Horm Behav.* 54, no. 1: 185–93.

If you do not have a regular menstrual cycle, it is highly recommended to check in with your doctor. Seeing a doctor allows you to rule out or address more serious health concerns that require medical treatment (cysts that need removal, thyroid problems, iron deficiencies, etc.).

Noteworthy Chemicals

Prostaglandins: While technically not hormones, these chemicals affect your body in a similar way. They are released from tissues in the body where there is an injury. They trigger an inflammatory response, and the muscles and blood vessels of the uterus start to contract.[3] **On Day 1 of your period, prostaglandin levels are high, and those levels decrease as the days go on.**

The Physical Process

The corpus luteum (a 2–5mm cyst on the ovary that releases the hormone progesterone to help build up the uterine lining) begins to dissolve, halting progesterone production (you'll learn about progesterone in the pages to come).

Estrogen production also decreases (you'll also learn about this hormone in the pages to come).

Prostaglandins are produced, causing muscle contractions in the uterus.

Contractions cause the uterine lining to be released through the vagina.

3 Inês Guimarães and Ana Margarida Póvoa, "Primary Dysmenorrhea: Assessment and Treatment," *Rev Bras Ginecol Obstet* 42, no. 8 (2020): 501-507.

Mind–Body–Earth Connection

Like a snake slithering into the shadows, hiding away to shed its skin, you are leaving an old part of yourself behind. It is time to release what no longer serves you. With the natural world as our guide, we can trust that transformation happens through shedding what has been outgrown.

Your blood is a sign that your womb is resetting itself, preparing for a new cycle. It is also a sign that you are undergoing an emotional reset. You will soon feel energized, focused, and confident, but you must first release the life burdens, the unhelpful thoughts or habits, the grudges, or whatever else no longer serves you.

Journal Prompt

Reflect on what you have outgrown. Is there an emotion that you are ready to release? Is there something in your environment that you want to let go of? What needs to be released so that your dreams can become a reality?

Activity: Meaning in Menstruation

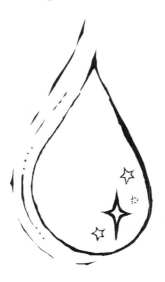

The sight of blood is powerful. It is the human lifeline, but when it flows out of the body, we also see death. Menstruators experience a truth of the natural world: everything that lives must eventually die. Menstruators can produce life, but every month they don't, they experience a death of sorts.

Most menstruators associate some of their strongest feelings and memories with the vibrant red liquid released within them each month. Your period blood may remind you of when you first began menstruating when you wore those white pants to school, or when a non-menstruator told you to be quiet about it, or of all the messes around your house you feel you need to clean up but have no time to. Some menstruators have the devastating reminder of a past miscarriage when they see their blood. Seeing blood is rarely associated with pleasant memories, especially in a culture that does not honor menstruation.

In this first activity, you will explore your personal associations with menstruation through amplification. Amplifying the experience of bleeding during your period may give you a chance to uncover what memories and associations might be influencing you right now. Amplification can illuminate emotional triggers that may lie in the unconscious mind, beneath the surface of your awareness.

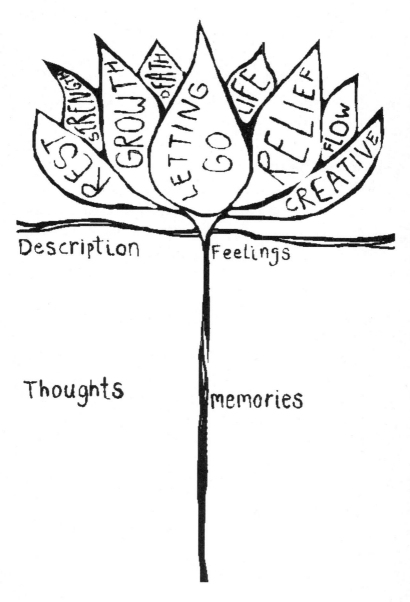

Beneath the lotus, write down what you associate with period blood. Describe your experience, record your feelings and thoughts during your period, and retrieve any memories that first come to mind. Are your associations empowering? Do any of them make you feel guilty or ashamed? Then, notice the words written in the lotus flower, and consider how they may be similar or different from your associations.

I am releasing...

During this menstrual phase, what associations with menstruation need to be released for you to build a more positive relationship with yourself? Write down what needs to be released in the blood drop labeled "1."

You will add to this image during each of your following periods and record what you hope to release in the numbered blood drops.

The Renewal: Follicular Phase

Cycle Day #

Ahhh the trouble-free follicular phase. The phase when work becomes effortless and accomplishing is second nature. Welcome to the phase of your cycle when the part of your brain responsible for learning, completing tasks, and controlling your thoughts is activated![4]

The Timeline

The follicular phase marks a new beginning after having just completed a full menstrual cycle. It begins at the start of

---

4 See Belinda Pletzer, Ti-Anni Harris, Andrea Scheuringer, and Esmeralda Hidalgo-Lopez, "The Cycling Brain: Menstrual Cycle Related Fluctuations in Hippocampal and Fronto-Striatal Activation and Connectivity during Cognitive Tasks," *Neuropsychopharmacology* 44, no. 11 (2019): 1867–75; Esmeralda Hidalgo-Lopez, Peter Zeidman, Ti-Anni Harris, Adeel Razi, and Belinda Pletzer, "Spectral Dynamic Causal Modelling in Healthy Women Reveals Brain Connectivity Changes along the Menstrual Cycle," *Communications Biology* 4, no. 1 (2021): 954; and Stephanie C. Reed, Frances R. Levin, and Suzette M. Evans, "Changes in Mood, Cognitive Performance and Appetite in the Late Luteal and Follicular Phases of the Menstrual Cycle in Women With and Without PMDD (Premenstrual Dysphoric Disorder)," *Horm Behav.* 54, no. 1: 185–93.

your period and lasts until halfway through your cycle, when ovulation occurs. If you have a 28-day cycle, the follicular phase lasts until around Day 14.

Although you are technically in the follicular phase when you bleed, begin the renewal phase of this book when you stop bleeding. Feelings of renewal usually sink in when you have released your blood (and whatever else needs to be released).

Noteworthy Hormones

Follicle-Stimulating Hormone (FSH): FSH releases from the brain and communicates to the ovaries that it is time to develop follicles where eggs can mature.

Luteinizing Hormone (LH): LH releases from the brain and communicates to the ovaries that it is time to release estrogen. LH is associated with increased sex drive and a positive mood.[5]

Estrogen/Estradiol: Releases from the ovaries and sends messages to the brain, signaling the release of other hormones. Estrogen promotes collagen production and creates plump, firm skin.[6] It is also associated with the part of the brain that increases cognitive functioning.[7]

5 W. H. Meller, K. M. Zander, R. D. Crosby, and G. E. Tagatz, "Luteinizing Hormone Pulse Characteristics in Depressed Women," *The American Journal of Psychiatry* 154, no. 10 (1997): 1454–55.

6 Amanda L. Clark, Ov D. Slayden, Kevin Hettrich, and Robert M. Brenner, "Estrogen Increases Collagen I and III MRNA Expression in the Pelvic Support Tissues of the Rhesus Macaque," *American Journal of Obstetrics and Gynecology* 192, no 5 (2005): 1523–29.

7 Esmeralda Hidalgo-Lopez, Peter Zeidman, Ti-Anni Harris, Adeel Razi, and Belinda Pletzer, "Spectral Dynamic Causal Modelling in Healthy

The Physical Process

Gonadotropin-releasing hormone (GnRH) is released from the brain.

GnRH triggers FSH and LH to be secreted from a different part of the brain.[8]

FSH causes follicles to form in the ovaries.

LH signals for the ovaries to release estrogen.

Eggs develop and mature in the follicles.

One dominant follicle houses the egg that will eventually be released.

Estrogen is low early on in the follicular phase and increases each day until ovulation.

Mind-Body-Earth Connection

Like the moon shining full, the tree expanding its roots, or the butterfly taking flight, this is your time to expand! You have finished a full cycle and released what you no longer need. Enjoy this period of renewal.

The hormones that help you develop eggs in your ovaries also communicate with your mind. They say, "Get out of the house and go find someone to make a baby with!" You might not want to make a baby though—understandable.

Women Reveals Brain Connectivity Changes along the Menstrual Cycle," *Communications Biology* 4, no. 1 (2021): 954.

8 Notice that these hormones are literally being released from your brain.

Instead, you can channel these hormones into saying, "I'm going to get out of my comfort zone, connect with people, and accomplish my goals!"

Journal Prompt

It is time to unleash your potential! What part of yourself do you want to grow into or expand?

Activity: Spread Your Wings

Now that your period is over, your hormones are working together to make you feel more energetic, social, and happy. Let this be the week that you go after the tasks you have been avoiding. Plan the trip you've been meaning to take. Try out a new exercise class. Connect with the friends you haven't made enough time for.

Ritual

Write in the wings of the butterfly what you plan to accomplish this week.

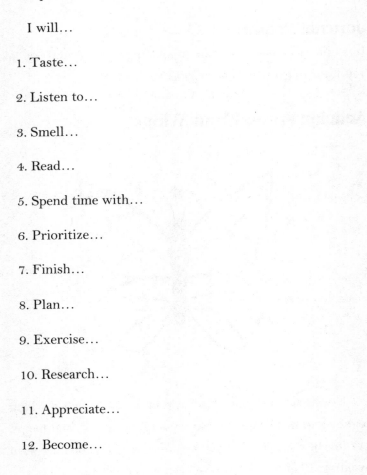

I will...

1. Taste...

2. Listen to...

3. Smell...

4. Read...

5. Spend time with...

6. Prioritize...

7. Finish...

8. Plan...

9. Exercise...

10. Research...

11. Appreciate...

12. Become...

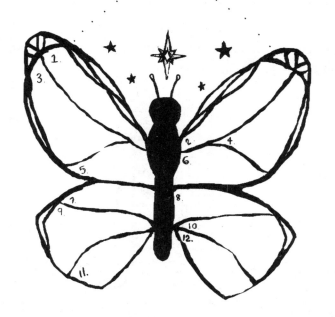

I am becoming...

During your follicular phase, you were given a chance to feel refreshed and renewed. Write down a word to describe what you discovered about yourself in the root labeled "1." During each cycle, you will add to the roots.

The Call: Ovulatory Phase

Cycle Day #

If you notice yourself having a shift in energy, after a period of feeling productive and focused, this may be a sign that your hormones are surging and dropping, inevitably influencing your mind. Ovulation has arrived! Even though you may have been dedicated and inspired to diligently complete a project at work, you may suddenly not care about it anymore. Your attention is shifting away from what you have been focusing on for the last week or two. It is time to shift your attention elsewhere.

Leading up to ovulation, your vaginal discharge may have a creamy texture. When your discharge becomes more like a raw egg white, wet and stretchy, you are likely in the ovulatory phase.[9]

9 Michael Zinaman, "Using cervical mucus and other easily observed biomarkers to identify ovulation in prospective pregnancy trials," *Paediatr Perinat Epidemiol* 20, no. 1 (2006): 26-9.

Some people can tell when their egg is being released from their ovaries because one side of their stomach will hurt (called mittelschmerz). This pain may be from the follicle bursting or the egg breaking through the wall of the ovary and entering the fallopian tube.

If you want to know for sure when you enter this phase, consider using ovulation test strips. These strips will let you know when your luteinizing hormone surges before the egg is released.

The Timeline

Ovulation happens halfway through the cycle. For a 28-day cycle, ovulation occurs about 14 days after the first day of the previous bleed. The process of ovulation—when the egg breaks through the ovary—is brief, lasting 12–32 hours. However, the drastic shift in hormones to prepare for ovulation might last several days.

Noteworthy Hormones

Testosterone: Releases from the ovaries and helps trigger ovulation. Testosterone increases sex drive and the intensity of orgasms.

The Physical Process

Estrogen, LH, and FSH sharply increase to reach their peak.

The surge in LH stimulates the ovaries to get ready to release an egg.

This spike in LH and FSH together causes the dominant follicle to get ready to burst and release an egg.

Right before the egg bursts (ovulation), LH, estrogen, and FSH decrease.

The egg breaks through the ovary and moves down the fallopian tube to the uterus.

Mind-Body-Earth Connection

Like the caterpillar weaving its cocoon, you are being called to grow your wings. Like a seed being covered in soil, you are in transition, preparing to grow deeper roots. Will you accept the call to focus away from the demands of the world and towards yourself?

Journal Prompt

What has inspired you lately? What new aspects of yourself or your life do you hope to tend to and grow?

Activity: Accept the Call

Halfway through your cycle, hormones start acting like a pin ball machine, shooting up and down through your body. You may suddenly feel unfocused, moody, or uneasy. Hello ovulation!

In the culture that surrounds you, it can feel easier to commit to long exhausting days at work than to commit to taking care of your own needs. Accepting the call to take care of our body and inner self is one of the ultimate challenges. Do you have the flexibility to loosen up your restrictive diets, intense exercise regimens, late nights with friends, long hours at work, and extensive study sessions? Can you sacrifice some productivity so that you can focus on you?

It is not actually unproductive to focus your energy inward and onto yourself. It will give you the ability to attune to your own needs, values, and wants. It will give you space to step back, look at your life, and consider whether you are living in a way that is aligned with your values and passions. It can help you to consider whether you are using your energy productively or if you are just wasting time.

Ritual

Agree to let go of the stressors that have been weighing on you by filling out this contract with yourself.

Mind–Body Contract

Commitments and expectations I will pause:

_____

_____

_____

The energy I normally put towards these stressors, will now go towards:

_____

_____

_____

I choose to do these activities this week (circle the practices that will help you build self-compassion):

Walk

Barefoot

Draw or paint

Do a loving-kindness meditation

Garden

Play music, sing, and dance

Talk with a therapist

Hike to a scenic overlook

Practice belly breathing

Prepare a nutritious meal with intention

Journal about an event or memory

Record a voice memo

Take a yin yoga class

Wash, exfoliate, and moisturize

Gently stretch

Do a visualization meditation

Sit by a natural water source

I _____ agree to accept the call of my body.

Signature: _____ Date: _____

I am called toward...

During your ovulatory phase, you have been called to give attention to the sides of yourself you try to ignore. What part of yourself or your life do you need to give more attention to? Write it in the voice of the conch shell labeled "1." During each cycle, you will add to each of the swirling lines of the conch shell's call.

The Descent: Luteal Phase

Cycle Day #

Here we go—it's time for the luteal phase. The luteal phase gets the worst rap. There is a lot going on in your body, your uterine lining is building up, and you probably feel bloated. Your body is going through it, preparing for the possibility of growing a new life inside your womb.

It's time we talk about progesterone, the hormone that allows your uterine lining to build up during this phase. This hormone should produce an anti-anxiety hormone called allopregnanolone, which should help you to feel calm through this phase.[10] However, in the presence of major

10 M. Schumacher, C. Mattern, A. Ghoumari, J.P. Oudinet, P. Liere, F. Labombarda, R. Sitruk-Ware, A.F. De Nicola, and R. Guennoun, "Revisiting the Roles of Progesterone and Allopregnanolone in the Nervous System: Resurgence of the Progesterone Receptors," *Progress in Neurobiology* 113, (2014): 6–39.

stressors, progesterone can get converted into cortisol.[11] Too much cortisol will make someone feel depressed and irritable.

In addition to progesterone increasing during this time, melatonin (the hormone that regulates your sleep) secretion changes.[12]

You may also notice food cravings or changes in appetite. This is because, during the luteal phase, your body has lower levels of leptin,[13] a hormone that regulates your weight.

During their luteal phase, most people also experience a sense of weight gain, abdominal bloat, or water retention. This is because the hormone plasma aldosterone increases, which helps sodium circulate through the body.[14] The more sodium you have consumed around this time, the more you will experience this water retention.

Also during this phase, your hormones will become out of balance if you drink excessive caffeine or alcohol, are put

11 Alexandra Ycaza Herrera, Shawn E. Nielsen, and Mara Mather. "Stress-Induced Increases in Progesterone and Cortisol in Naturally Cycling Women," *Neurobiology of Stress* 3 (2016): 96–104.

12 A. Shechter, P. Lespérance, N. M. K. Ng Ying Kin, and D.B. Boivin. "Nocturnal polysomnographic sleep across the menstrual cycle in premenstrual dysphoric disorder," *Sleep Medicine* 13, no. 8 (2012): 1071–1078.

13 Chih-Hung Ko, Cheng-Fang Yen, Cheng-Yu Long, Yu-Ting Kuo Cheng-sheng Chen, & Ju-Yu Yen, "The :Late-Luteal Leptin Level, Caloric Intake and Eating Behaviors among Women with Premenstrual Dysphoric Disorder," *Psychoneuroendocrinology* 56, (2015): 52–61.

14 Emily D. Szmuilowicz, Gail K. Adler, Jonathan S. Williams, Dina E. Green, Tham M. Yao, Paul N. Hopkins, and Ellen W. Seely, "Relationship between Aldosterone and Progesterone in the Human Menstrual Cycle," *The Journal of Clinical Endocrinology & Metabolism* 91, no. 10 (2006): 3981–87.

under stress, exercise too much or too little, or if you have disordered eating.

If you do not track or understand what is going on in your body, you may feel completely out of control during this time. This can create a spiral of dark thoughts, self-deprecation, suicidal ideation.[15]

With everything that is physiologically fluctuating in your body, the part of your brain that picks up on physical sensations will become hyperactive. For some menstruators, this part of their brain looks like someone's brain who is having a post-traumatic stress response.[16] This is a sign that the body is carrying trauma.

If you are under a lot of stress—including being stressed out about your fluctuating body during this phase—the part of the nervous system that helps with heartbeat and breathing starts to decrease its functioning too.[17] When the body is stressed, all those necessary bodily processes stop responding like normal.

15 C. E. Pilver, D. J. Libby, and R. A. Hoff. "Premenstrual Dysphoric Disorder as a Correlate of Suicidal Ideation, Plans, and Attempts among a Nationally Representative Sample," *Social Psychiatry and Psychiatric Epidemiology* 48, no. 3 (2013): 437–446.

16 See Corey E. Pilver, Becca R. Levy, Daniel J. Libby, and Rani A. Desai, (2011). "Posttraumatic stress disorder and trauma characteristics are correlates of premenstrual dysphoric disorder," *Archives of Women's Mental Health*, 14(5), 383–393, as well as Amit Etkin and Tor D. Wager, "Functional Neuroimaging of Anxiety: A Meta-Analysis of Emotional Processing in PTSD, Social Anxiety Disorder, and Specific Phobia," *The American Journal of Psychiatry* 164, no. 10 (2007): 1476–1488.

17 Tamaki Matsumoto, Hiroyuki Asakura, and Tatsuya Hayashi, "Biopsychosocial Aspects of Premenstrual Syndrome and Premenstrual Dysphoric Disorder," *Gynecological Endocrinology* 29, no. 1 (2013): 67–73.

To sum it up, the luteal phase has the potential to cause overwhelming physical sensations which can cause the brain to feel reactive, like it is responding to a threat. This is why it is so valuable to track your cycle and become aware of how your hormones are affecting your mood, physical sensations, and behaviors. Once you learn to listen to your body, you can begin to nurture it rather than feel threatened by it.

The Timeline

The luteal phase begins after ovulation and lasts until you get your period. In a 28-day cycle, this phase occurs in the 14 days before you bleed. Premenstrual syndrome (PMS) may occur in the last few days of this phase, the late luteal phase.

Noteworthy Hormones

Progesterone: Progesterone releases from a cyst (the corpus luteum) that forms on an ovary after ovulation. It helps maintain a thick uterine lining through relaxing the muscles in the uterus so that early contractions do not occur. When under emotional stress, progesterone is associated with increased emotional reactivity.[18] When in balance, it produces anti-anxiety affects.[19]

---

18 Alexandra Ycaza Herrera, Shawn E. Nielsen, and Mara Mather, "Stress-Induced Increases in Progesterone and Cortisol in Naturally Cycling Women," *Neurobiology of Stress* 3 (2016): 96–104.

19 M. Schumacher, C. Mattern, A. Ghoumari, J.P. Oudinet, P. Liere, F. Labombarda, R. Sitruk-Ware, A.F. De Nicola, R. Guennoun, "Revisiting the Roles of Progesterone and Allopregnanolone in the Nervous System: Resurgence of the Progesterone Receptors," *Progress in Neurobiology* 113, (2014): 6–39.

Estrogen: Works with progesterone to build up the uterine lining. Low estrogen is linked to PMS symptoms.

Leptin: Regulates weight and appetite. Lower levels cause food cravings.

Aldosterone: Regulates flow of sodium through the body. It causes water retention in the stomach, ankles, and breasts.

The Physical Process

FSH and LH stop being released (these are the hormones that helped your body grow and release an egg).

A cyst called the corpus luteum grows on your ovary.

This cyst forms in place of the burst follicle that released an egg.

Progesterone releases from the corpus luteum.

Progesterone prepares your womb for the potential of your egg being implanted and creates a healthy uterine lining by preventing muscle contractions.

Progesterone production causes aldosterone to increase, which increases the sodium circulating through your body.

Sodium circulation causes water retention (breast tenderness, bloat, and swollen ankles).

Estrogen levels rise to build up the uterine lining.

The uterine lining stays intact if the egg gets implanted in the uterine lining.

The uterine lining will be released if the egg is not implanted.

Mind–Body–Earth Connection

Like the caterpillar in its cocoon metamorphosing into a butterfly, the luteal phase is when you descend into your own quiet hiding place. Your body needs a period of silence and solitude.

Like the darkness of the new moon, you may not be able to see the way that you shine during this phase. It's okay though: you do not need to shine for others. It is instead time to give attention to your shadow self, the dark or hidden parts of your being you may prefer to ignore.

Journal Prompt

During the descent, your hormones might make you become critical of whatever is around you. Do not dismiss or judge yourself during this phase. Ask instead, "What in my life is hindering or threatening my creative potential?"

Activity: Your Shadow Self

Every menstruator has a shadow side. Your shadow side may resemble Ursula from The Little Mermaid, the witch who was shunned away in a deep ocean trench—angry, brewing potions, and scheming. When family crosses your boundary and requests yet another favor, resentment may begin to boil inside you. When work demands more of your time and energy than you have, you may find it harder and harder to comply. In this way, cultural conditioning creates an angry witch in most, if not every, menstruator. Have you gotten to know your inner witch?

Cutting off and rejecting this side of you will only bring about shame, self-deception, self-criticism, depression, anxiety, and other emotional symptoms. The anger every menstruator has is likely rooted in fears, traumas, or valid frustrations associated with being a menstruator in a patriarchal culture. The challenge is in learning to accept this side of yourself. Descend into your darkness and embrace it. You likely have a reason to be angry.

Ritual

This activity is intended to be completed when you are actively experiencing PMS. It most likely feels uncomfortable right now, but try to compassionately bring attention to your body. Sit down on the floor and consciously feel each of your limbs, starting with your feet and scanning up towards the crown of your head. Using the sensation list, record the sensations you feel in the part of your body that experiences them. You can also use colors and symbols to convey what you feel.

As you give attention to these feelings in your body for several minutes, what feelings or thoughts do you notice? Don't try to change any of these feelings. Just let them be.

achy	dizzy	jumpy	shudder
airy	dull	knotted	silky
alive	elastic	light	smooth
bloated	electric	loose	soft
blocked	empty	moist	spinning
breathless	energized	moving	sticky
brittle	expanding	numb	still
bubbly	faint	open	stretchy
burning	flaccid	paralyzed	stringy
buzzy	fluid	pounding	tender
chilled	flushed	pressure	tense
clammy	flutter	prickly	thick
closed	frantic	puffy	throb
cold	frozen	pulled	tickly
congested	full	pulsing	tight
constricted	furry	quaking	tingling
contracted	gurgling	quiet	trembly
cool	hard	quivering	twitching
cozy	hot	radiating	vibration
comfortable	heavy	ragged	warm
contracted	icy	raw	winded
cool	intense	rolling	wiggly
cozy	itchy	shaky	wobbly
crampy	jagged	sharp	
damp	jittery	shimmering	
dense	jumbly	shivery	

I give myself space to deepen into...

During your luteal phase, record what feeling you recognized and felt. Write down a word to describe what you deepened into on the wave of the whirlpool labeled "1." During each cycle, you will add to each of the lines that form the tendrils of this whirlpool.

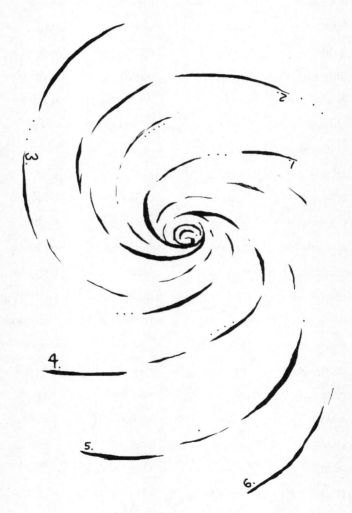

Cycle Two: Follow the Symbols

Throughout this cycle, you are invited to pay special attention to the images that resonate with you throughout your cycle. In each phase, different images or symbols may spark your curiosity or grab your attention. Images may show up around you, like the hummingbird outside of your window. They may show up in your thoughts, like the memory of your childhood home. They may emerge in your fantasies, like imagining becoming a famous singer. They even might appear in your dreams at night. You will be guided to bring meaning to these images, transforming them into symbols.

Symbols are reminders of your wisdom. They offer inspiration to guide you forward. Living a life where you see symbolically can bring you meaning and invites a connection between you and the world around you.

You can start by looking through your social media or phone. Pay attention to what aesthetic you are drawn to or what images you want to look up. You might try looking around your house and noticing what decorations you like. Do you like house plants? Quilts? Crystals? You may pay extra attention to song lyrics you want to listen to over and over, or a book you can't stop reading. Do they paint a picture in your mind that you are attracted to? Start to consider what these specific images mean to you.

The Body as a Symbol

Your body itself can carry symbolism. The stomach, for example, has been said to symbolize the containment of feelings. The chest has been said to symbolize feelings of self-worth and power.[20] The image of a breast has been said to symbolize life source.[21] But what matters more than what these images are said to symbolize is asking yourself, What do these images symbolize to me?

Scan your body and notice the sensations you experience. What body area is your attention drawn to? What do you associate with this part of your body? What story does this part of your body want to share?

---

20 Erik Jarlnaes and Josette van Luytelaar, *Body Breath and Consciousness: A Somatics Anthology*, (Berkley: North Atlantic Books, 2004), 263.

21 Ami Ronnberg and Kathleen Martin. *The Book of Symbols*, (Köln: Taschen, 2010), 388.

The Symbols Nature Offers

It can be especially meaningful to notice how the natural world offers symbols that relate to the menstruating body. The forest fluctuates through seasons, like the phases of the menstrual cycle. When the forest becomes overworked by human behavior, like through logging, farming, or climate change, it will lose its balance. Animals will suffer, plants will die, and wildfires might take over. When the menstruating body is overcontrolled, put on a restrictive diet, or overexercised, the hormones of the body will also lose their natural balance.

Other cultures, in the world and throughout history, have used symbols of the natural world to deepen their connection to their body. The phases of the moon and ocean tides, for example, have been used as powerful symbols for menstruators, teaching them to look outside of themselves, to better understand and connect to the rhythm of their body.

Cycle Two Task

In Cycle One, you learned about the physiological processes of the menstrual cycle and you practiced connecting your thoughts and behaviors with these processes. In Cycle Two, you will use your knowledge of what is happening within your body to recognize how it connects with what happens in the world outside of your body. You may notice the tree's leaves falling off the tree, releasing like the blood you shed. You may notice a flower blooming, like your follicles do after your period. Your menstrual cycle mimics the creative processes around you, and, this month, your goal is to notice and gather symbols to help bring you meaning and inspiration throughout your journey.

The Release: Menstrual Phase – Cycle Two

Cycle Day #

Sheds Life, but Still Lives

When a snake grows, it finds a place to hide away and shed the skin that it no longer fits in. This process has made the snake a symbol of growth and rebirth in cultures throughout the world. The snake's transformation process shows us that we must shed old parts of ourselves to grow. The womb also teaches this as it sheds a lining each month to prepare for a new cycle.

Though snakes are also associated with deadly venom, hissing, and slithering, these creatures use their unique strengths to thrive. They cannot hear, but they can sense vibrational frequencies that other animals cannot.

Menstruators also have a special ability: their intuition. Studies show that the part of the brain in charge of accessing memories and future imaginings becomes activated during the menstrual phase.[22] This makes it the ideal time to trust your intuition. Let go of the past and move into the future.

Shedding the uterine lining can be painful. It may bring out sides of you that are like a hissing, venomous snake, but this phase does not make you weak or make you a problem. It leads you towards a renewed self, one that can emerge from hiding as a stronger, more developed version of you.

As you bleed, let your vibrant red liquid serve as a reminder of the parts of you that you have outgrown.

Ritual

Follow the directions below to consider the different parts of yourself. Like a snake releasing its skin or the blood you are currently shedding, is there a part of yourself that can be released? Consider any negative self-views, unhealthy coping strategies, or persistent guilts you may be experiencing that no longer serve the growing version of yourself.

22 Elizabeth Osborn, Anja Wittkowski, Joanna Brooks, Paula E. Briggs, & P. M. Shaughn O'Brien, "Women's Experiences of Receiving a Diagnosis of Premenstrual Dysphoric Disorder: A Qualitative Investigation," *BMC Women's Health* 20, no. 1, (2020), 1–15.

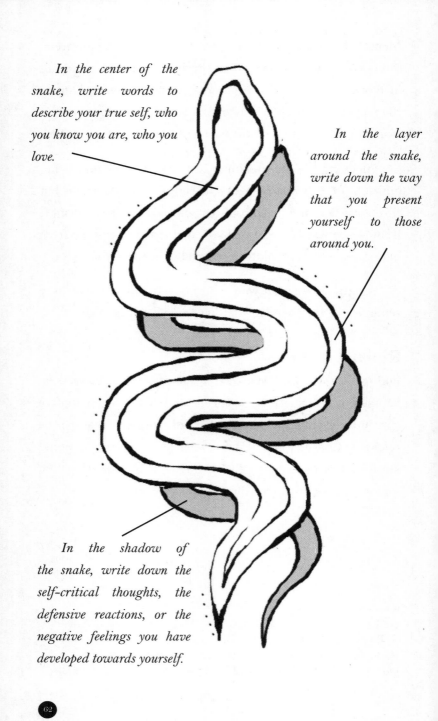

In the center of the snake, write words to describe your true self, who you know you are, who you love.

In the layer around the snake, write down the way that you present yourself to those around you.

In the shadow of the snake, write down the self-critical thoughts, the defensive reactions, or the negative feelings you have developed towards yourself.

I am releasing...

Write down what things you emotionally released during "Cycle One" in the blood drop labeled "1" on page 31. Check in with yourself: have you been able to let whatever it is go? Or are you still working on releasing it from your life?

During this new cycle, what do you choose to release so that you can grow, like a snake shedding its skin? Write it down in the blood drop labeled "2."

The Renewal: Follicular Phase – Cycle Two

Cycle Day #

Symbol of the Soul

The leader of analytic psychology, Carl Jung, developed the concept of individuation. He theorized that each person's lifelong task is to realize and become their most authentic self. This means bringing consciousness to parts of the self that have been rejected by family and culture, or parts of the self that have been repressed due to trauma or fear. Once aspects of the true personality are realized, Jung suggested that the goal is to then integrate these qualities into your way of being in this world, becoming less fragmented and more whole.

Each follicular phase offers an ideal opportunity for you to experience yourself growing and expanding, or individuating. You may feel lighter now after menstruation. Your hormones are activating your energy levels and focus abilities. You may be able to see the full version of yourself more clearly right now. In this activity, you will gather symbols that inspire you to realize and become this version of yourself.

Ritual

Sit comfortably and think about a time recently that you felt most like yourself. This might be a time when you had a focused state of mind, a time when you were able to communicate openly, or maybe a time when you were seen and loved for your unique qualities. Whatever it was, let yourself sit with this memory in your mind. Feel free to journal about the moment.

After you think about this for a few minutes, notice the feelings in your body.

Place symbols, colors, drawings, or magazine images in and around the womb space part of the image to represent this memory of yourself. Let your imagination run freely. Keep checking back in with your body as you complete this drawing.

After doing this activity, choose a symbol that showed up in your imagination. Maybe you drew a feather, a nicely cooked meal, or an animal. Let this symbol represent your soul. Write it down below your picture.

Soul Symbol: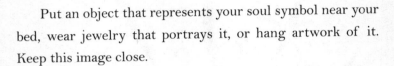

Put an object that represents your soul symbol near your bed, wear jewelry that portrays it, or hang artwork of it. Keep this image close.

I am becoming...

Record your self-discovery from Cycle One on the root labeled "1" on page 38. Now consider the symbol that you discovered in the exercise you just completed. What does the symbol say about who you are becoming? Write it in the root labeled "2."

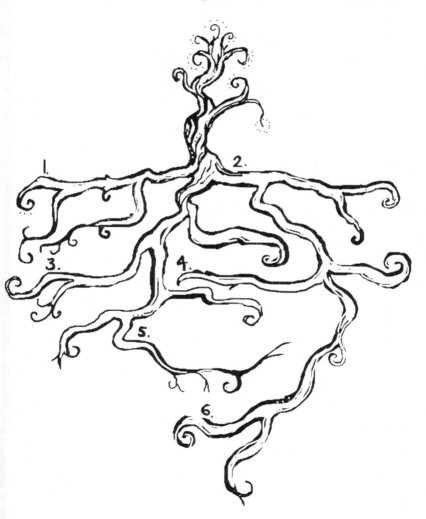

The Call: Ovulatory Phase – Cycle Two

Cycle Day #

Activity: The Cosmic Egg

The Cosmic Egg is a symbol in many creation myths that represents self-expansion and spiritual growth.[23] During ovulation, an egg—that contains the power of creation—is released within your womb. Let this egg represent the desires that you want to manifest and bring into reality.

As your body goes through ovulation, your attention may be pulling you in a direction you were not expecting it to. Try to remain open and curious to where your focus might shift to. There are parts of yourself that want to grow, but these parts may seem mysterious and unknown to you right now.

---

23 Ami Ronnberg and Kathleen Martin, *The Book of Symbols*. (Köln: Taschen, 2010), 14.

Ritual

Create a vision of your future self and creative aspirations. Consider what has been making you feel excited. Notice what on social media has captivated you recently. What fantasies have you had? Inside of the egg, draw or paste images or items, and/or creatively write. What are you being called to channel your creative energy towards?

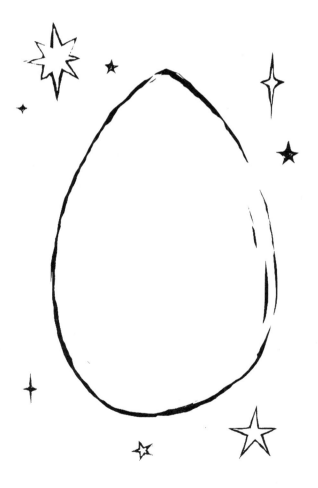

I am called toward...

What were you called to during Cycle One? Write it down where it is labeled "1" on page 46. Now, add what you are being called toward in the voice of the conch shell labeled "2."

The Descent: Luteal Phase – Cycle Two

Cycle Day #

Wildfire Womb

During the luteal phase, it is normal to feel angry. Hormones are raging and your body may feel like a water balloon about to pop...of course you're mad. Attempting to ignore rage oftentimes just fuels more rage.

What you're experiencing during the luteal phase is like a wildfire. It's natural, it's smothering you, and it feels out of control. People fear natural wildfires, just like people fear a menstruator's valid anger.

You would think that when people see a wildfire, they should just put it out. However, wildfire experts have learned that putting out small wildfires results in the forest becoming overgrown. When the forest gets overgrown, larger fires eventually erupt catastrophically. Larger fires later emerge and destroy everything in their path, even the hundreds-of-year-old trees.

If we compare the natural luteal phase experience to fire, we know that the more the feelings of anger are suppressed, the more likely they are to eventually erupt and burn everything down. Give yourself permission to let your anger burn with the force of a small, uncontrolled wildfire. Trust that it will help to clear out what does not belong.

This does not mean you have a free pass to be mean to others or yourself. Instead, this means you have permission to let your anger exist and be there, without judgment or a need to respond to it.

Ritual

Visualize a fire burning in the forest, clearing away small trees and brush, leaving only the strongest trees with the thickest bark still standing alive. Can you continue to visualize a wildfire in your mind, without judging it as bad? Can you instead see it as an opportunity for rebirth and renewal? Wildfires in nature are the catalyst for transformation. Your anger can also become your catalyst for inner transformation.

Inside of the flame, write down the anger you are currently experiencing. During this luteal phase, what in your life may need to be burned down? Outside of the flame, write down what in your environment you hope is still standing strong after your fiery emotions are felt.

I give myself space to deepen into...

Where it is labeled "1," record what you deepened into during Cycle One on page 56. Add to the whirlpool the fiery feelings you deepened into in Cycle Two where it is labeled "2."

Cycle Three: Your Animal Nature

*T*he poet Mary Oliver overcame a history of abuse through seeking solace in the natural world. In her powerful poem "Wild Geese," she wrote about how our goal is not some arbitrary standard of goodness but only to treat our animal bodies well. Mary Oliver calls out the experience many of us have—overworking and striving to be better and better. And she challenges that way of living, offering the profound idea that maybe we are allowed to just let our bodies be. With Mary Oliver as your inspiration this cycle, you are going to practice viewing your body as though it contains an inner animal that needs to be nurtured and protected.

The Animal of Your Body

Your physiological systems, such as the menstrual cycle, have evolved over thousands of years, perfecting their functions to best ensure your survival. Your thinking, imaginative brain cannot control this part of you. Your body still will respond like a wild animal, with ravenous food cravings when it has been starved or by becoming hyperalert when it hears a strange noise at night. Just like we cannot control the reactions of our pets, we cannot control the way our body responds to the environment. What we can do is control how we treat it. We can talk to it when it feels panic and remind it that it is safe. We can feed it when it is hungry.

Imagine your womb as an animal, curled up on your stomach. Which animal would it be? Would you give it enough water each day and feed it the freshest food you could? Or would you starve it? Would you give it time to relax? Or would you put the animal to work all day? Is your animal living a life of abundance or is it just trying to survive the day?

If an animal doesn't have its basic needs met, it will be hyperalert to its surroundings. The slightest change in the environment will send it into fight or flight. This cycle, you will pay attention to how well your inner animal is surviving.

The Ego

You live in a body, but also have a mind that is conscious and able to make rational decisions in alignment. This part of your mind tries to make decisions that align best with your sense of self, referred to as the ego. Ideally, your ego makes choices that nurture the animal of your body so that the animal can exist peacefully, carrying out bodily functions with ease (breathing, digesting nutrients, sleeping through the night, etc.).

Animal-Ego Disconnect

Your ego may want to be seen as healthy, but then you binge-eat several cookies after eating a salad. Your ego may want to be productive and successful, but then you end up napping all day. Your ego may try to always appear sweet and kind, but then you become irritated and snap at everyone in your path. When you act in a way that you believe is out of alignment with your ego, that might mean your animal's basic needs are not being met. Your animal might feel threatened and feel the need to retaliate against your ego.

Threats to the Animal

When animals are starving, they pursue prey they would otherwise avoid. When animals are under attack, they fight back or run away. Captive animals often struggle to reproduce, and they lose their natural menstrual cycles.

The animal within you reacts to similar threats too. Restrictive diets, dependency on caffeine or a substance, high stress, or overexercising are all threatening. These factors are all linked to disruption of menstrual cycle hormonal flow from the animal-like region of the brain.[24]

When your animal brain is disrupted, your ego will lose strength. You might get the sense that you are out of control, like something greater than you has taken over and is calling the shots. This is the animal of your body telling you it is scared.

Survival Mode

When the animal of the body senses a threat, it is likely to go into survival mode. Survival mode will override your ego, and you will struggle to find the strength to make intentional decisions. With the menstrual cycle, survival mode urges may look like an impulse to excessively eat, to obsessively ensure safety, to oversleep, to be hypercritical of everyone, or to be hyperalert throughout the night. These urges are a sign that your animal needs to be nurtured.

Victim to the Animal

Imbalanced menstrual cycle hormones can feel like they are taking over your life. They can feel like a wild animal taking over, calling all the shots, victimizing you. Trust that in learning how to nurture the animal within, you will no longer feel like a victim to it.

---

24 "Pathophysiology of Functional Hypothalamic Amenorrhoea in Women Subject to Psychological Stress, Disordered Eating, Excessive Exercise or a Combination of These Factors," *Clinical Endocrinology* 95, no. 2, (2021), 229–238.

Cycle Three Task

In the previous cycle, you practiced viewing your cycle as something more meaningful than just a physiological process. During Cycle Three, you will continue to think symbolically, seeing your physical form like an animal that you are responsible for.

You will start to care for the animal of your body by considering if there are any habits you have that are hurting it. You will consider how you can live a productive life, while giving your body time to rest and digest. You will consider what needs you have that you may be ignoring and you will take space away from others so that you can really listen to the voice of your inner animal.

The Release: Menstrual Phase – Cycle Three

The Threatened Animal

This menstrual phase, you are guided to look honestly at the actions that your ego has developed. Sometimes the ego develops habits to defend itself against shame. Oftentimes, defensive actions do not nurture the body.

Do any of your actions cause the animal of your body to lash out? Some habits that your ego may develop to protect you from shame can cause hormonal imbalances.[25]

Habits Formed by the Ego	Response of the Threatened Animal
Restricting food, eliminating food groups, dieting	Intense food cravings, food obsession, binge eating, weight fluctuation
Overexercising	Low energy, mood swings, missed period
Drinking excessive caffeine	Hormonal depletions and spikes, morning fatigue, anxiety
Drinking alcohol	Mood swings, irritability, dependence

25 Amy Morrison, Suszanna Fleming, Miles Levy, "A review of the Pathophysiology of Functional Hypothalamic Amenorrhoea in Women Subject to Psychological Stress, Disordered Eating, Excessive Exercise or a Combination of These Factors," *Clinical Endocrinology* 95, no. 2, (2021). 229–238.

Ritual

You are invited to begin releasing whatever habit does not support the harmony between your ego and animal. Be honest and compassionate with yourself. Releasing behaviors that have been a part of your life will be a journey full of low points and peaks, but do not give up. Have compassion: you are just beginning.

Habit Formed by the Ego:

What purpose has this habit served?

How does this habit threaten the animal within your body?

Why do you want to release this habit?

Visualize in detail what your life would be like if you did not have this habit.

When do you feel most tempted to engage in this habit?

Who can support you in the process of releasing this habit?

What habit can you form to replace your current habit?

I am releasing...

In the blood drops labeled "1" and "2," record what you released during your earlier cycles in the blood drops on pages 31 and 64. Write down the habit that you will release now in the blood drop labeled "3."

The Renewal: Follicular Phase – Cycle Three

Cycle Day #

Harmony

During each renewal phase, you may notice you become more productive and energetic. The part of your brain that plans, memorizes, and controls mental tasks becomes activated.[26] Your ego might feel strong and in control. To ensure that your animal and ego remain in harmony, consider how you can work towards achieving your goals, while also nurturing your body.

26 Esmeralda Hidalgo-Lopez,, Peter Zeidman, Ti-Anni Harris, Adeel Razi, and Belinda Pletzer, "Spectral Dynamic Causal Modelling in Healthy Women Reveals Brain Connectivity Changes along the Menstrual Cycle," *Communications Biology* 4, no. 1 (2021): 954.

Ritual

Record in the sunrays what you hope to achieve this week. Record in the animal how you can also take care of your body. Make sure your goals don't conflict with your ability to nurture your body during this phase.

I will achieve...

I will Nurture...

I am becoming...

Record the ways you have grown in previous cycles on pages 38 and 69. What part of yourself are you growing now? Write it in the root labeled "3."

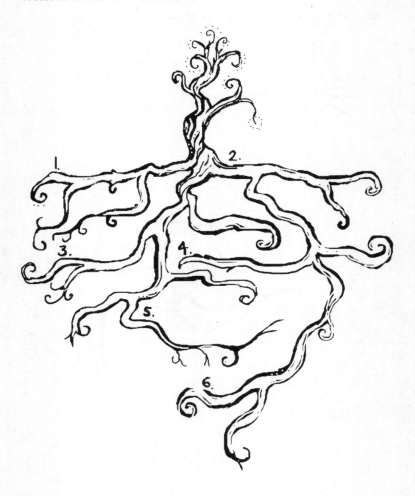

The Call: Ovulatory Phase – Cycle Three

Cycle Day #

The Call to Nurture

As you ovulate this cycle, the creative strengths of your mind and body can guide you towards new approaches to managing emotional stress. During the phase that follows ovulation, your body will let you know if it hasn't been well nurtured. Now, you are being called to start nurturing your inner animal before it screams at you.

As you are called into the luteal phase, try to never discount your emotions by saying, "It's just PMS." Do not take on the cultural belief that your emotions are "crazy." Your emotions are not invalid. Treating them like they are will only make the animal within scream at you louder, demanding more and more of your attention. Prepare to give your emotions even more room to be processed and expressed. Let them take up as much space as they ask for so that they can move through you. You are being called to take care of your body and mind, to nurture yourself so that your menstrual cycle can follow its natural rhythm.

Ritual

The root of your emotions often will lead you to the medicine you need. In this activity, let yourself deepen into what is causing you emotional distress so that you can better understand what your soul needs.

In the waves, imagine the ocean, which symbolizes the depths of emotion. You are being called to jump in and learn about your inner world. For each number in the waves, answer the corresponding prompt:

What has triggered you to feel emotional distress recently?

How did you react?

Think deeper: what feelings did you have in that moment?

Ask those feelings, "What do you need right now?" Do they need space to just be? Do they need comfort? Do they need to be listened to?

Once you have filled out all the lines in the waves, consider how you can take care of the part(s) of yourself that may need help.

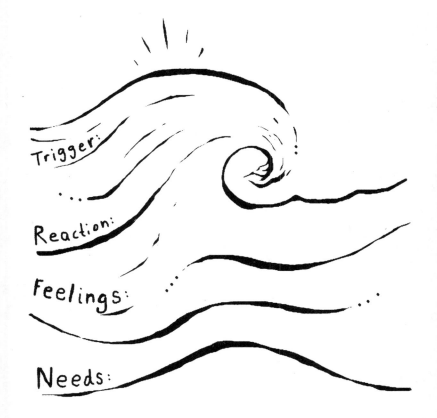

Trigger:
...

Reaction:

Feelings: ...   ...

Needs:

I am called toward...

What have you been called towards in previous cycles (see page 46 and 72)? Record them in the blanks labeled "1" and "2." What do you feel called towards now? Write it in the voice of the conch shell labeled "3."

The Descent: Luteal Phase – Cycle Three

Cycle Day #

Cocoon

If the animal within your body is threatened, it will let you know now. During the luteal phase, you might receive hormonal urges to eat in excess if you have been undereating. You might be crippled with fatigue if you have been overworked. If it seems like your body is turning against you, this is the luteal phase's way of telling you what it needs. Listen.

If it is not a baby you are creating this luteal phase, consider what else you are hoping to create and if there is anything in your environment preventing you from being able to create what you envision.

Ritual

Use the blanks in the cocoon illustration to create a journal cocoon around yourself so that you can listen and honor the voice of your body. Where will you sit? What objects will you gather to create a sense of comfort and peace? Is there an affirmation you can speak? Bring a book and journal with you. Dedicate time for inner reflection in this space as often as you need throughout the descent.

I give myself space to deepen into...

Record the words that describe your previous descents in the waves labeled "1" and "2" of the whirlpools on pages 56 and 76. Consider what you have deepened into in Cycle Three. Write it on the wave of the whirlpool labeled "3."

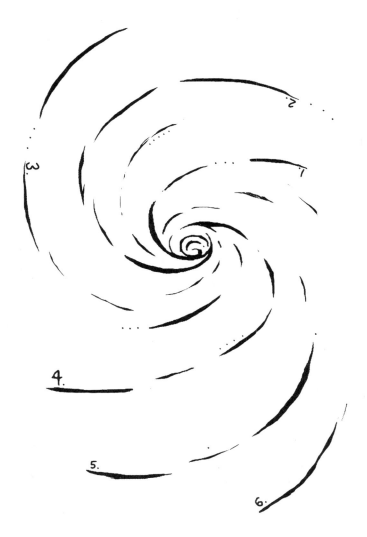

Cycle Four: The Womb and the Patriarchy

Principles of the Patriarchy

A patriarchy is a culture where masculine norms dominate and men more often hold positions of power. A patriarchy creates an ego-driven society. The soul of the society gets lost as people strive relentlessly for personal achievement, power, and control. The natural world gets swept away and menstruator's natural bodies lose their natural flow.

In a patriarchal culture, the needs of the menstruating body are not widely taught or understood. Menstruating people often become constricted and controlled, confined to act within societal expectations. Patriarchal culture encourages goal-driven development, rigidity, routine, control, and emotional repression, emphasizing wealth building and ladder climbing. These principles can of course serve a purpose in anyone's life. However, overvaluing these cultural principles will cause the menstruating body to become neglected.

Overvaluing Patriarchal Principles

Overvaluing career success can cause excessive stress. Overvaluing physical fitness can cause someone to stop eating intuitively. Patriarchal standards tend to silence emotions and silence the voice of the body. They disrupt hormonal harmony. The patriarchy seeks control and tells the wildness within every menstruator that it is not welcome.

Being threatened from living in a patriarchal environment, the wild animal of the menstruating body lives in a survival mode and tends to lash out in response to patriarchal standards. It begs for 12 hours of sleep a night, it stays hyperalert all day, it lashes out emotionally when it is silenced too long, and it binges on chips and ice cream after going all day without eating enough.

When the luteal phase hits, the menstruator who has followed patriarchal pressures too rigidly might feel victimized, chaotic, out of control, or exhausted. Their inner animal is scared, and society doesn't care.

To care for your inner animal, you can learn to embrace what the patriarchy has rejected: stillness, introversion, emotions, relationships, and your changing body. If your feelings or behaviors feel out of control, debilitating, or dominant, especially right before having your period, you may be too strictly following patriarchal norms. Recognizing how societal pressures have caused the animal within you to feel threatened is a step towards learning how to make your body a safe home. You deserve to feel safe in your body.

Cycle Four Task

At this point, you have learned what is physiologically occurring in your body, how your menstruating body relates to the world around you, and how you can treat your body with care and nurturance. Your body is like a vulnerable animal for you to protect and cherish. Part of protecting your body is learning to stand up against the patriarchy so that you can keep it safe.

In Cycle Four, you will acknowledge how patriarchal values may be affecting your body and your emotional well-being. You will reconsider what values need to be prioritized so that you can live more in sync with your body. You will also practice finding alternative approaches to living in a patriarchal world.

The Release: Menstrual Phase – Cycle Four

Cycle Day #

Dancing in the Flames

Many patriarchal principles prevent menstruators from feeling connected with their physical form and the full range of their personality. When your body is bleeding, it naturally resists nearly everything that patriarchal culture promotes. The menstrual cycle asks for flexibility, tolerance of discomfort and pain, compassion, respect for emotions, and so much more that is culturally devalued.

Ritual

The following list includes some of the principles that are heavily promoted in our culture. Highlight the principles that you currently chase after. Are there any that you attempt to follow, but consistently fail to achieve? This may be a sign that you are overvaluing something that is not natural to you. This may be a sign that the patriarchy has influenced you in a way that is unauthentic to your true self.

Patriarchal Values

Accuracy	Individualism	Privacy
Achievement	Industry	Purpose
Attractiveness	Luxury	Rationality
Authority	Order	Rigidity
Conformity	Perfectionism	Self-Control
Efficiency	Pleasure	Structure
Extraversion	Popularity	Tidiness

I overvalue... _____

Ritualize the Release

Write down any inauthentic values to yourself on a piece of paper. Then burn it. After burning the paper, reflect on these questions:

How does it feel to burn this expectation of yourself?

What fears do you have in releasing this value from your life?

What purpose has valuing this principle served?

I am releasing...

Record what you released in previous cycles (see pages 31, 64, and 85). Then record what patriarchal standard you have chosen to release this cycle in the blood drop labeled "4."

The Renewal: Follicular Phase – Cycle Four

Cycle Day #

Explore Your Values

As you enter the follicular phase, you are entering the time of the month when you may find it easier to focus on planning, learning, and structured thinking. As this phase progresses and concludes, your body and mind will ask that you switch focus. The productivity, social energy, or clarity that you feel now may disappear. You are on a cyclical path and so your growth will happen like a spiral, not a straight line. Do not get too attached to the level of productivity that you might experience now.

Ritual

Highlight the principles in the following chart that may enable you to capitalize on the brain strengths of your follicular phase and allow you to work towards achieving your goals.

To experience the deepest growth, you must take time to step away. Choose a different color, then highlight what principles may allow you to descend inward and have productive downtime. Productive downtime offers you the rest your body and mind crave.

Acceptance	Creativity	Growth	Mindfulness	Risk
Accuracy	Dependability	Health	Moderation	Romance
Achievement	Duty	Helpfulness	Monogamy	Safety
Adventure	Ecology	Honesty	Non-conformity	Self-Acceptan•
Attractiveness	Efficiency	Hope	Nurturance	Self-Control
Authority	Excitement	Humility	Openness	Self-Esteem
Autonomy	Extravagance	Humor	Order	Self-Knowledg•
Beauty	Extraversion	Independence	Passion	Service
Caring	Faithfulness	Industry	Perfectionism	Sexuality
Challenge	Fame	Inner peace	Pleasure	Simplicity
Change	Family	Intimacy	Popularity	Solitude
Comfort	Fitness	Justice	Power	Spirituality
Commitment	Flexibility	Knowledge	Privacy	Stability
Compassion	Forgiveness	Leisure	Purpose	Structure
Conformity	Friendship	Loved	Rationality	Tidiness
Contribution	Fun	Loving	Realism	Tolerance
Cooperation	Generosity	Luxury	Responsibility	Tradition
Courtesy	Genuineness	Mastery	Rigidity	Wealth

I am becoming...

In the roots labeled "1" through "3," record the ways you have been renewed in previous cycles on pages 38, 69, and 88. Add the principles that resonated with you most during this phase in the root labeled "4."

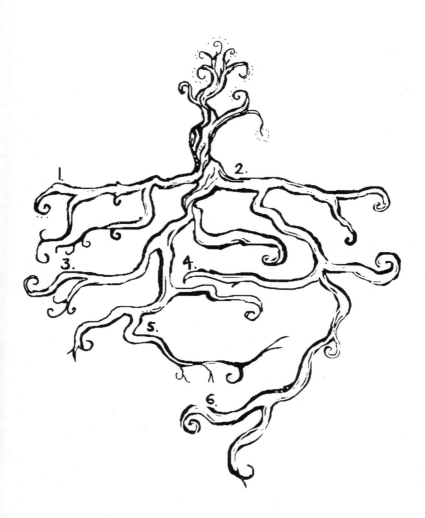

The Call: Ovulatory Phase – Cycle Four

Cycle Day #

Find Your Voice

Studies show that the part of your brain responsible for writing, reading, and speaking functions best during the ovulatory phase.[27] During this phase, you are being called to develop your empowered voice.

Ritual

Give a voice to how the patriarchy has impacted you. Has living in a patriarchal society caused you to diet, exercise, or have a negative body experience? Has it misguided the direction of your career or academic pursuits? Have others around you expected you to behave in a way that doesn't feel authentic to you? Fill the following page with words and phrases that communicate the impact it has had in your life.

---

27 Esmeralda et al, "Predicting Ovulation from Brain Connectivity: Dynamic Causal Modelling of the Menstrual Cycle," *bioRxiv* (2020): 2020–08.

I am called toward...

What have you been called towards in previous cycles (see pages 46, 72, and 92)? Write them down in the blanks labeled "1" through "3." What do you feel called towards now? Write it in the voice of the conch shell labeled "4."

The Descent: Luteal Phase – Cycle Four

Cycle Day #

The Power of the Opposite

During the days before getting their period, menstruators often report feeling like they are in a battle with their body or their mind. They want to feel sexy or act productively, but something blocks them from feeling that way. Patriarchal culture pressures menstruators to want a small stomach, a positive attitude, and a productive mind, but the body demands something else. This is the great tension that menstruators experience.

You have a cyclical body yet live in a linear culture. You may want to go sit on a bench in the park and read, but your boss is demanding you meet a 4:00 PM deadline. Can you feel the tension of your body and your culture pulling away from each other? The following ritual will allow you to uncover what may help you move through this tension and into a life that is more aligned with your authentic self.

Ritual

Confront a conflict you have recently or currently experienced by completing the following activity. Consider if this conflict is occurring because of patriarchal pressures for you to act or be a certain way. Once you complete the activity, hold the image that emerges close to you. Use it as a symbol of how you can stand up to patriarchal pressures.

Find a comfortable spot to sit alone. Let your mind wander to the thing that is most distressing to you right now, the thing that you are worried about the most.

Connect your stressor to something that reminds you of a similar feeling. For example, your workload may remind you of drowning in the ocean. Or maybe your messy house

reminds you of a landfill. The feeling in your body may feel like a stallion wanting to break free from its stall. Draw, collage, or write about this image. Let your imagination run the show.

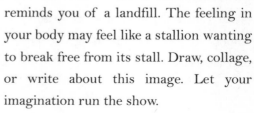

How do you feel in your body as you artistically express your picture?

Now, look around you. Notice what is on the walls or in the air, notice any smells, notice what you can hear.

Refocus. Imagine, what is the opposite of the image you just created? Swimming in the ocean might be the opposite of drowning. A 5-star hotel room might be the opposite of a landfill. A flying bird might be the opposite of a trapped stallion.

Incorporate this new image into your drawing, collage, or writing.

How do you feel in your body while working with this new opposite image?

I give myself space to deepen into...

Label your previous descents in the waves of the whirlpool (see pages 56, 76, and 95). Consider what you are being called to deepen into now. Write it on the wave of the whirlpool labeled "4."

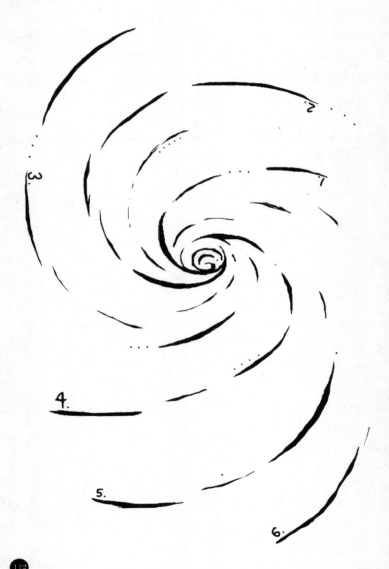

Cycle Five: Trauma in the Body

s of a study published in 2024 by Child Abuse and Neglect, 31.6% of menstruators experience childhood sexual abuse.[28] It takes having a strong support system and consistent professional help to face the outrageous cruelty of sexual abuse. What happens to those who don't have support? What about those who don't feel safe enough to tell anyone at all? Many menstruators end up directing their shame and pain inward. They blame themselves. It might feel easier to blame their body than their perpetrator. By the time many menstruators reach adulthood, they have lost the ability to feel safe in their own body.

---

28 David Finkelhor, Heather Turner, and Deirdre Colburn, "The Prevalence of Child Sexual Abuse with Online Sexual Abuse Added," *Child Abuse and Neglect*, no. 149, (2024).

When menstruators stop trusting their body, anything that affects their body can feel like a threat, even the natural fluctuations of the body. Physical sensations can trigger memories and emotions from when they were abused. They might simply be stretching or eating and become activated with memories or associations of their abuse. Sexual abuse can cause the physical sensations associated with the menstrual cycle, especially during the premenstrual phase, to become a threat.

Cultural Abuse

All menstruators are prone to experiencing cultural abuse, which happens when patriarchal culture objectifies, ostracizes, and taboos menstruators for being in their body. Pornography often depicts menstruators in victim roles, portraying them as helpless and abusable. Politicians, most of whom don't even have a uterus, will set restrictions on what menstruators can and cannot do with their body. Many role models that menstruators look up to follow strict diets and alter their body through invasive cosmetic procedures. There are countless examples of the culture we live in sending abusive messages to menstruators.

Cultural abuse is so ongoing and disturbing that it can feel easiest to just ignore it. But, ignoring it only allows it to become more powerful over you. For example, the health and wellness industry sends subtle messages that menstruators need to buy new products, exercise plans, medicines, and procedures. This industry is widespread and now engrained in our culture. It is manipulative, making menstruators feel bad about themselves so that they can be convinced to buy products that make them feel better about themselves. Ignoring how this is oppressive causes menstruators to fall deep into this trap. Unfortunately, the trap will never lead to feeling the peace, confidence, or whatever else the menstruator might be seeking.

Trauma and the Luteal Phase

As discussed, many menstruators have trauma associated with their physical body. Therefore, when their mind becomes more aware of their physical body during the luteal phase, they might be reminded of their physical traumas.

There is a formal diagnosis in the Diagnostic and Statistical Manual of Mental Disorders (DSM-5), the bible that mental health professionals use to diagnose mental health disorders, for those who have severe emotional symptoms related to the menstrual cycle. Premenstrual Dysphoric Disorder (PMDD) is when premenstrual symptoms take over to the point where the menstruator feels out of control, emotionally reactive, unstable in their relationships, and suicidal.[29] Menstruators

29 Elizabeth Osborn, Anja Wittkowski, Joanna Brooks, Paula E. Briggs, and P. M. Shaughn O'Brien, "Women's Experiences of Receiving a Diagnosis of Premenstrual Dysphoric Disorder: A Qualitative Investigation," *BMC Women's Health* 20, no. 1, (2020), 1–15; C. E. Pilver, D. J. Libby, and R. A. Hoff, "Premenstrual Dysphoric Disorder as a Correlate of Suicidal Ideation, Plans, and Attempts among a Nationally Representative Sample," *Social Psychiatry and Psychiatric Epidemiology* 48, no. 3 (2013): 437–446; Tory Eisenlohr-Moul, Madeline Divine, Katja Schmalenberger, Laura Murphy, Brett Buchert, Melissa Wagner- Schuman, Alyssa Kania, Sabina Raja, Adam Bryant Miller, Jordan Barone, and Jaclyn Ross, "Prevalence of Lifetime Self-injurious Thoughts and Behaviors in a Global Sample of 599 Patients Reporting Prospectively Confirmed Diagnosis with Premenstrual Dysphoric Dsorder," *BMC Psychiatry*, no. 199, (2022): 1–15.

who fit the description of PMDD often report having suffered trauma in their past.[30] The brain activity of someone with PMDD (specifically, hyperactive activity in the insular cortex) even mimics the brain activity seen in people with post-traumatic stress disorder.[31]

Meeting the diagnostic criteria of PMDD does not mean you have a pathological illness that you're stuck with forever. It does not mean you require medication. It likely means that you have not been given the proper tools, support, and coping strategies to feel safe during the luteal phase. If your premenstrual symptoms are so severe that you feel suicidal or severely depressed, seek out a therapist trained in addressing trauma stored in the body.

Cycle Five Task

Throughout the past four cycles, you learned about how your body naturally ebbs and flows. These physical fluctuations keep you fertile and creative. The phases offer wisdom. During this cycle, you are going to be gently prompted to consider how past abuse may prevent you from fully honoring the wisdom of your body. Then, you will try to release it.

30 Corey E Pilver, Becca R Levy, Daniel J Libby, and Rani A Desai, "Posttraumatic Stress Disorder and Trauma Characteristics Are Correlates of Premenstrual Dysphoric Disorder," *Archives of Women's Mental Health 5*, no. 14, (2011): 383–393.

31 Amit Etkin and Tor D. Wager, "Functional Neuroimaging of Anxiety: A Meta-Analysis of Emotional Processing in PTSD, Social Anxiety Disorder, and Specific Phobia," *American Journal of Psychiatry 10*, no. 164, (2007): 1476–1488; Gingnell et al., "Menstrual Cycle Effects on Amygdala Reactivity to Emotional Stimulation in Premenstrual Dysphoric Disorder." *Hormones and Behavior 4*, no. 62, (2012): 400–406.

If you are safe in your current living situations and have a few people around you who can support you, you will be asked to revisit some of the abuse you have been through. Once you are safe enough to fully feel the weight of what has happened to you, you can practice letting it move out of you. You can make conscious choices to stand up against it, and you can give yourself the support that no one gave you at the time.

As mentioned, the experience of one's body can trigger painful memories and post traumatic responses. When exploring the symptoms of the menstrual cycle, it is strongly recommended to have a support system and therapist to hold you through the content that arises.

Cycle Day #

Blood of Medusa

There is a Greek myth that tells a story of Medusa, a once beautiful priestess who was raped by one of the gods. She was punished for it by being given snakes for hair and cracked skin. Then, she was cast away onto an island and forced to live there alone. The only people who would come to her island were men trying to kill her. If these men looked her in the eyes, she would turn them to stone.

To this day, victims of sexual assault often receive harsher blame and punishment than do the perpetrators. Menstruators who "tempt" men are shamed, while men are not held responsible for their own actions. How do victims ever learn to trust again? After what happened to Medusa, why would she ever want a guy to look at her again? Maybe it was better that they all just be turned to stone.

It was a sad way to live, always alone and in fear. Then, one day, Medusa was killed. From her blood, the majestic winged horse Pegasus emerged. Medusa's power of turning men to stone had to be sacrificed before what she was harboring within her could be revealed.

Medusa is a symbol of a protective shield after experiencing abuse. Her blood is a symbol of sacrificing the need to live overly protective and in fear. Finally, Pegasus is a symbol of the freedom and healing that comes from eventually surrendering a protective shield that is no longer needed. As you bleed, consider if you have any protective shields that no longer serve you and hold you back from living the life you want to live. What would it be like if you sacrificed those shields?

Ritual

Freely color, write, and draw around the image of Medusa as you consider the following questions:

What abuse have you faced that you continue to fear?

How have you learned to protect yourself from it happening again?

With your period blood as your inspiration, imagine what may need to be sacrificed, so that you can become free. . .

I am releasing...

In the blood drops labeled "1" through "4," record what you released in the menstrual phases of the previous cycles in this book (see pages 31, 64, 85, and 101). In the blood drop labeled "5," write what you plan to release now.

The Renewal: Follicular Phase – Cycle Five

Cycle Day #

Your Inner Child

During the follicular phase, you have an opportunity to reintegrate parts of yourself that have become hidden over the years. As you grew up, you may have learned which of your personality traits were acceptable and unacceptable and which behaviors were desired and rejected based on your gender. Traumatic experiences can cause kids to bury sides of themselves.

The child who had confidence speaking in front of an audience may have lost it when someone made fun of their outfit. The child who dreamed of becoming a successful business owner may have lost the dream when they began working long hours as a nanny. Consider: What did you know about yourself as a kid that you may have forgotten about? Are you safe enough now to bring rejected sides of yourself back?

Ritual

In this phase of renewal, try to bring awareness to the childhood sides of yourself that you may enjoy bringing back into your personality. If you are worried that the culture that surrounds you may not approve of these qualities, try to find a safe space to practice expressing these sides of yourself. Use the following questions as journal prompts to guide you on this journey.

How would you describe your childhood personality?

What images, toys, activities, or games were you drawn to as a child?

What parts of your childhood self do you still notice in yourself today?

Which qualities might be worth intentionally bringing back into your personality?

How might you reawaken these sides of you?

I am becoming...

In the roots labeled "1" through "4" record how you have been renewed in previous cycles (see pages 38, 69, 88, and 105). In the root labeled "5," add how you are being renewed now.

The Call: Ovulatory Phase – Cycle Five

Cycle Day #

Voice of the Body

With ovulation, your hormones are peaking and dropping. As your body fluctuates, you are being called to accept the fluctuation, rather than to reject it. Most menstruators notice discomfort within their body during or after ovulation. Whether it is a bloated belly, difficulty sleeping, or achy breasts, you are being called to compassionately surrender to your experience.

To begin accepting your body for the way it naturally ebbs and flows through phases, complete this ritual as often as you wish. Find a safe space to attune to your body experience. Notice what feels uncomfortable, what feels strong, and whatever else feels alive in your body. Is there a part of your body you want to escape from? Are you able to compassionately notice your body, or do you notice negative self-talk?

Ritual

After you bring awareness to your body for a few minutes, color the body below. Choose a color to use on the parts of your body that you feel comfortable with. Use another color for the parts of your body you are uncomfortable with.

If these parts of your body could speak, what would they say? What can you do to comfort these parts of your body?

I am called toward...

What have you been called towards in previous cycles (see pages 46, 72, 92, and 108)? Record them in the blanks labeled "1" through "4." What do you feel called towards now? Write in the blank labeled "5."

1.
2.
3.
4.
5.
6.

...

The Descent: Luteal Phase – Cycle Five

Cycle Day #

Self-Soothe

During the luteal phase, managing PMS happens through intentionally creating calmness and building practices to soothe the inner unease. Self-soothing strategies are necessary to have during the phase of descent.

Some menstruators become self-critical, self-harming, or ashamed of themselves during their luteal phase because of the uncomfortable symptoms that surface. Shame and self-criticism cause stress. Stress only exacerbates hormonal symptoms and creates a cycle of self-destructive tendencies. Learning to practice self-compassion and acceptance during the luteal phase will give you the strength to flow with your body's rhythm, even if it is bringing you into the depths.

Ritual

In this exercise, you will bring the distressing symptoms of PMS out into the open, through sculpture. By facing the discomfort, you can explore how you will meet your premenstrual symptoms with nurturance, compassion, and acceptance.

Materials:

Moldable medium (clay, sand, dough, mud, etc.)

Water

Space to work with medium

Time:

30 minutes

Task:

Consider a difficult stressor you are currently experiencing in your luteal phase. This could include stomach discomfort, relationship tension, or impulsive eating—anything that you are hung up on right now.

Think about the images you associate with this symptom. Think metaphorically. Stomach bloat, for example, may give you the image of a balloon that is about to pop.

With your moldable medium, use your imagination to mold the medium to represent the image. You may incorporate other objects you find into your creation.

Look at what you molded. This is a physical representation of your stressor. Your stressor can now be held in your hands. How can you change this shape so that it no longer causes you distress? What does the shape need?

Journal or reflect: How do you feel now that you have remolded your stressor? How might remolding the clay inform how you respond to the stressor in real life?

I give myself space to deepen into...

Write the themes of your previous descents in the waves labeled "1" through "4" of the whirlpool (see pages 56, 76, 95, and 112). Consider what you have deepened into now. Write it on the wave labeled "5."

Cycle Six: Victim No More

Victim Archetype

Sometimes people blindly start acting out an archetype. Archetypes are acted out when someone's behaviors, thoughts, decisions, and feelings mimic the exact patterns of fictional characters in film, art, and literature. Acting out an archetype isn't authentic; it is acting in the way someone is pressured or conditioned to act.

If you think about popular shows and books throughout history, menstruators are often portrayed as a victim. Think of Greek mythology, for example. Women in these myths often marry young and become secluded in their household by their husbands. They become a victim to their circumstance.

Menstruators have too often been portrayed as having no power to change their situation.

When menstruators feel out of control, in a society where they are also told they are out of control and seen as out of control, they are at risk for acting out the victim archetype.

As an example, the medical world tends to medicate menstruators when they feel out of control of their emotions before they have their period, rather than educating and empowering them. If medication works for you, that is a great solution. If it does not work, consider if being told to take medicine feels dismissive of your experience. Taking medicine for menstruating may feel victimizing. People who experience behavioral and emotional fluctuations with their cycle might not need medicine; they might need to be heard and validated. They might need to feel empowered to reclaim the parts of themselves they have felt ashamed of in a patriarchal world. They might need education so that they can learn to listen to the needs of their body.

From Victim to Empowered

A bloated belly is only a problem when living in a culture that makes people think they need a flat one. Resting is only a problem in a culture that obsesses over productivity. Emotions are only a problem in a culture where they are viewed as weak.

Becoming empowered requires you to create your own standards for yourself. You might need to give yourself permission to accept yourself, as you feel and are, right now.

Cycle Six Task

The moment someone accepts themselves is the moment they can accept how much power they have. You have practiced accepting the natural rhythm of your body. You have strategies now to accept even the most challenging symptoms that come with the cycle. You have accepted the wild animal of your body, rather than rejecting it. You have faced the frustrating impact the patriarchy has had on you as a menstruator, rather than ignoring it. Trauma and abuse have tried to beat out your authentic qualities, but you are practicing fighting back. Acceptance of the self is a constant process. It is also a necessary step in taking charge of your life.

This cycle you will practice releasing remnants of the victim archetype that have been projected onto you. This will allow you to complete your journey standing securely rooted in who you are, even with a fluctuating body. You will practice cleansing yourself of these victimizing thoughts, using the natural world to carry you. You will share your wisdom with others and truly recognize how powerful and creative you really are.

The Release Menstrual Phase – Cycle Six

Cycle Day #

Flow

It is your last period on this guided journey. This menstrual phase, give yourself permission to release the cultural pressures and mindsets that have made you feel victimized. What can you let go of? Your self-critical thoughts, culturally influenced standards, or food restrictions? Whatever holds you back, give yourself space to release it now.

Let the emotions run through you as you release what has weighed you down. Experience the feelings and then let them pass. When your emotions are not fully experienced, they will dam up. This dam may help you appear strong, but it does not help you thrive. Try catching the current of your emotional waters instead. As you let your stream carry you, do not judge yourself. Judging or resisting your emotions is like trying to swim upstream. Resisting the flow of nature is a losing battle.

Ritual

Sit next to a stream, take a shower, or watch a fountain or waterfall flow. Breath with the moving water. When you feel a sense of calm in both your mind and body, visualize the abuse, shame, or trauma you have experienced that has made you feel victimized. Journal about your experience.

In the river illustration, highlight the words that describe how you would feel if you were no longer a victim.

Tender

Adored ~ Secure
Encouraged ~ Clean ~ Alive ~ Playful ~ Silly

Trusting ...

Light ~ loved ~ Quiet
Happy ~ joyful ~ Clearheaded
Free ~ moved ~ Comfortable
Relaxed ~ Inspired ~ Serene ~ tranquil
hopeful ... Motivated ~ Still
Vibrant ~ Focused ... Refreshed
Creative ... Renewed ~ peaceful ~ Calm
healthy ~ strong ~ beautiful

137

I am releasing...

In the blood drops labeled "1" through "5," record what you released before (see pages 31, 64, 85, 101, and 121). In the drop labeled "6," write what you plan to release now.

The Renewal: Follicular Phase – Cycle Six

Cycle Day #

Together

Now that you have developed awareness of the ancient wisdom existing within your cyclical body, it is time you extend this wisdom beyond yourself. It is time for you to model how to stand up against the patriarchal system. You can also be a witness and supporter of other menstruators who are doing the same. You are ready to develop your empowered voice, see your power reflected through others, and lift others up.

A strange thing sometimes happens though. Sometimes menstruators do not support other menstruators. Sometimes competitiveness, rigidity, and/or comparison divides them. Another menstruator's accomplishments may feel difficult to praise. An older menstruator may withhold mentorship from a young menstruator in need of support. Some menstruators passively perpetuate cultural standards of beauty by overvaluing youthfulness (through using Botox, plastic surgery, or weight loss surgeries) and undervaluing the wisdom that comes with age. You have the power to change the oppressive force of the patriarchal culture. Pay close attention this week to your relationship with other menstruators in your life and in your past.

Because it is not easy to stand up against cultural norms, every menstruator needs support to become confident within their authentic self. Menstruators can become empowered through giving and receiving each other's love and validation.

Ritual

Use the social energy that comes with your follicular phase, in addition to the wisdom that you have found within yourself, to uplift others through any of the following activities.

Actions you can take to empower other menstruators:

Give flowers

Listen with no judgement

Assume positive intentions

Acknowledge accomplishments

Leave an uplifting comment on social media posts

Encourage what they are excited about

Model body positivity by showing confidence in your own body

Give compliments (not about appearance)

Introduce them to other menstruators you know

Buy from menstruator-owned businesses

Offer mentorship

Ask questions about their passions

Celebrate self-expression

Praise another for accomplishing their goals

This month I will support another menstruator by:

_____

I am becoming...

In the roots labeled "1" through "5," record who you have become in the previous cycles in this book (see pages 38, 69, 88, 105, and 124). In the root labeled "6," add who you are becoming now.

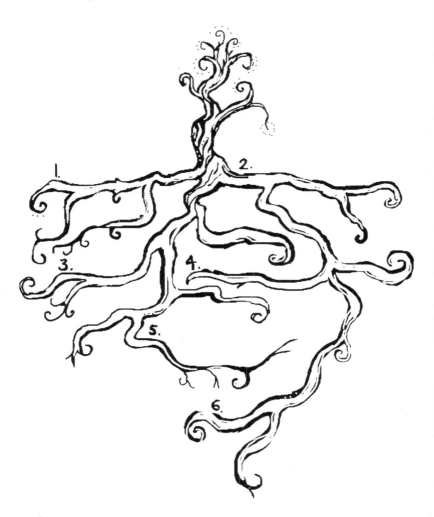

The Call: Ovulatory Phase – Cycle Six

Cycle Day #

Transcend

Over the course of five cycles, you have confronted the different sides of yourself. Do you notice tension between a side of yourself you are developing and a side of yourself that you used to be? In this ovulatory phase, you are being called to embrace this tension.

Sometimes you may catch yourself having conflicting values, goals, plans, desires, etc. You might desire to be free-spirited like someone you saw online, but also value your rigidity and routines. You might have dreams of speaking out about a cause you care about, but also always prioritize living within your comfort zone. Sometimes the goals you set are unachievable because of the tension between two different sides of yourself.

Consider the tension you are experiencing in your life right now. Let this tension exist without fighting it or taking action. Eventually, new thoughts or perspectives will emerge and allow you to transcend what is holding you back.

Ritual

Write down two contrasting attitudes, values, goals, plans, or thoughts—one in the moon and one in the sun.

Sit with the discomfort their conflicting energy creates.

Meditate on this for as long as you need. You may need to sit with the tension for minutes or for days.

In the cloud, record what new thoughts or ideas came up by holding the conflict in tension.

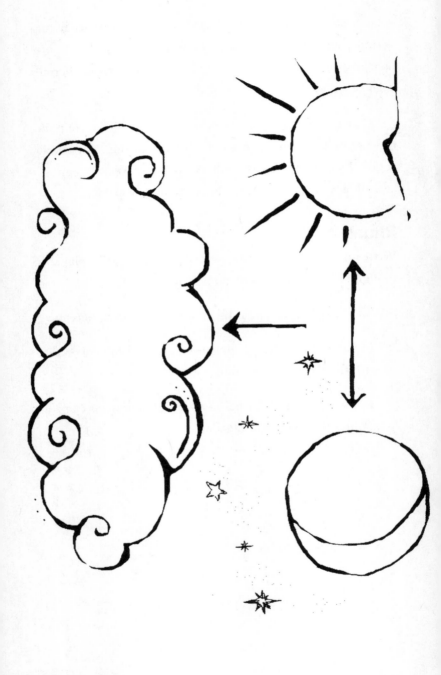

I am called toward...

What have you been called towards in previous cycles (see pages 46, 72, 92, 108, and 127)? What do you feel called towards now? Record each thing from the previous five cycles and this current one in the corresponding lines.

The Descent: Luteal Phase – Cycle Six

Cycle Day #

Phases of You

You are entering the last phase of your guided journey. Throughout these past six cycles, you have met new sides of yourself and you have revisited the old. You have been in touch with both the sweet and sour, warm and cold, tender and strong parts of yourself. You are becoming more aware of your whole, soulful self. Take this descent as an opportunity to reflect using the following ritual.

Ritual

Flip through this workbook and reflect on all the mini-journeys you went through to get to this point. Write within the spaces of the mandala on the following page the words that best describe all the different parts of you that you have discovered along the way.

I give myself space to deepen into...

Label your previous descents in the waves of the whirlpool (see pages 56, 76, 95, 112, and 131). Consider what you are being called to deepen into now. Write it on the wave of the whirlpool labeled "6."

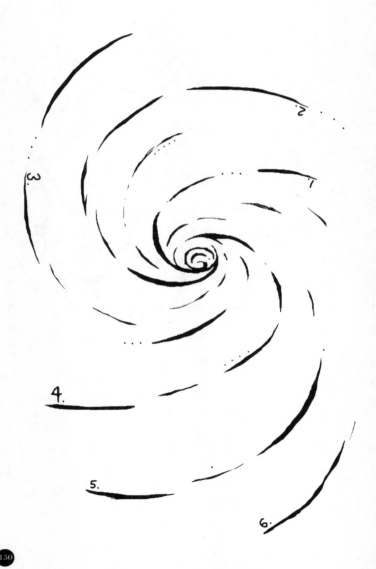

Concluding Activity: The Return

You have been guided through six mini-initiations towards becoming a more vibrant, soulful version of yourself. Each menstrual cycle offered an opportunity for you to block out the noise of the patriarchal culture around you, so that you could build a stronger connection to your body and to the cycles of the world around.

From here, your body will continue to ask you to listen to its aches, moods, pains, and urges. These symptoms are a reminder for you to descend inward and pay attention to your own needs. As you move through life, remember the wisdom of your body; find time to retreat inside before blooming outwards.

One day, your menstrual cycles will decrease frequency and eventually disappear. You will reach the final initiation: menopause. Your body will stop responding to cyclical hormones, and it will start to slow down. The vibrancy of youth that many menstruators associate with beauty will fade. What will always remain is your wisdom. Your wisdom and authenticity will radiate from your being. Your ability to defy societal standards and show up confidently as you are will be captivating.

This workbook has ideally taught you to live in flow with your body, rather than resisting its needs and desires.

Ritual

Take a step back and look at how far you have come since beginning this journey. Summarize your reflections over the past six menstrual cycles in this activity.

In the falling leaf, record what has been released.

Inside of the growing tree, record what has been renewed.

Inside of the seed, record what you have been called to.

Inside the water, record what has been descended into.

You are the hero; this was your journey. Now how will you return to day-to-day life with the wisdom you've gained from within your sacred cycle?

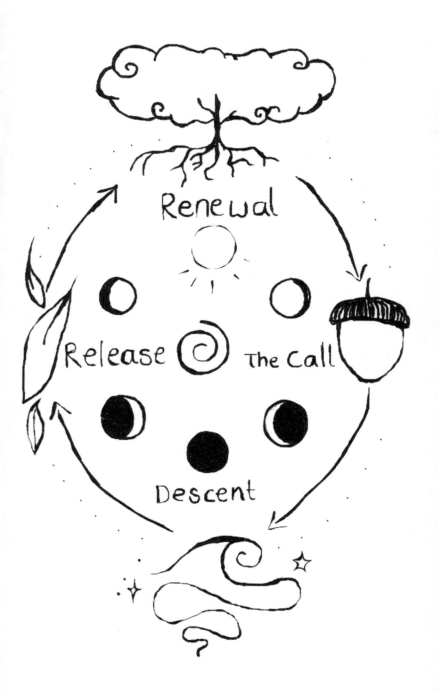

Renewal

Release

The Call

Descent

Additional Journal Pages

Additional Journal Pages

Additional Journal Pages

Additional Journal Pages

About the Author

Mary McDonald is a Licensed Clinical Professional Counselor in Montana, a California registered therapist, and a licensed teacher with master's degrees in counseling psychology and culturally responsive pedagogy. Mary studied depth psychology at Pacifica Graduate Institute, where she learned how psychological healing can occur through exploring the rejected and repressed parts of the self. She speaks about and specializes in treating people who struggle with women's issues including trauma, premenstrual syndrome (PMS), premenstrual dysphoric disorder (PMDD), and hormone imbalance. Using a feminist approach to psychotherapy, she has helped those who struggle with patriarchal oppression find their voice, strength, and inner wisdom. Through her own personal journey to work through PMDD, bulimia, and depression, she found that art, ritual, and depth therapy were necessary tools in empowering her to manage the side effects of hormonal imbalance. You can find her online at marymcdonaldtherapy.com.

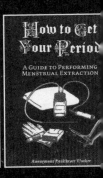